DEM☉S

Demos is an independent think tank committed to radical thinking on the long-term problems facing the UK and other advanced industrial societies.

It aims to develop ideas – both theoretical and practical – to help shape the politics of the twenty first century, and to improve the breadth and quality of political debate.

Demos publishes books and a regular journal and undertakes substantial empirical and policy oriented research projects. Demos is a registered charity.

In all its work Demos brings together people from a wide range of backgrounds in business, academia, government, the voluntary sector and the media to share and cross-fertilise ideas and experiences.

For further information and
subscription details please contact:
Demos
9 Bridewell Place
London EC4V 6AP
Telephone: 0171 353 4479
Facsimile: 0171 353 4481
email: mail@demos.co.uk

The family in question

Stein Ringen

DEM⊙S

First published in 1998
by Demos
9 Bridewell Place
London EC4V 6AP

© Demos 1998
ISBN 1 898309 69 8

Printed in Great Britain by EG Bond Ltd

About the author
Stein Ringen is Professor of Sociology and Social Policy at Oxford University and a Fellow of Green College. He is the author of a range of books and articles on social policy, inequality and social trends.

This book draws on research which is reported in more detail in *Citizens, families and reform* (Oxford University Press, 1997). Chapter four is a revised text of a public lecture delivered at Green College in Oxford on 1 May 1997.

Other publications available from Demos:

Family learning: the foundation of effective education
Relative values: support for relationships and parenting
Time out: the costs and benefits of paid parental leave
Parental leave: the price of family values?
The parenting deficit

To order a publication or
a free catalogue please contact
Demos (details overleaf).

Contents

Foreword

With this book I wish to encourage analysis of the late twentieth century social and family revolution. I believe the family remains an essential and productive institution for the well-being and freedom of the individual. I believe 'family values' are about rock hard issues of material standard of living and democratic citizenship, and about liberal ethics and equality of opportunity. I believe we are wrong to see the family as peripheral to modern life in advanced industrial democracies. I believe we have yet to understand how rapidly and radically the circumstances of family life are now changing. I believe these changes are at the cost of economic efficiency and social fairness in our societies.

My perspective is liberal. Free and rational citizens live in community with others. They know they need the guidance of community to live successful lives. Liberalism without community is libertarianism. I wish to shake my fellow liberals out of their libertarian complacency about the decline of the family.

Stein Ringen
Oxford, spring 1998

Summary

1. Family economy

In democratic societies, citizens have the freedom to seek life strategies which are useful to them in their quest for what they consider to be a good life. A condition for doing this with success is an adequate material standard of living. Our standard of living depends on the money economy (including government) and the family economy. In this equation, the importance of the family economy is underestimated because the methods we use for the measurement of standard of living consider only the money economy. The family is a business which adds value to what it purchases in the market. If we define the national economy as consisting of those activities which determine the material standard of living, half the national economy is family economy. Over recent decades, there has been a decline in the family economy while there has been growth in the money economy. Our material standard of living has therefore increased less than we are led to believe from income statistics of prosperity and growth in the money economy.

1. For a productive and efficient national economy, we should invest in the family as we invest in enterprises in the money economy. Economic policies go wrong if they neglect the family economy.
2. Mainstream economic statistics give us misleading information about the real standard of living and its trends and distributions. This distorts political debate and misdirects economic policy. Alternative and better methods of measurement are available and should be applied.

2. The cost of children

The raising of children is a job families do for society. All members of a society have a common interest in assuring the continuation of the population and in the raising of the next generation. Couples have children out of love and because children give them joy and meaning in life, but child rearing is also a job. There are costs involved in taking on this job. Children need housing, clothing, food, equipment, transportation and the like. Although such direct costs are considerable, and rising, they are not costs that worry parents. They are aware of these costs when they decide to have children and are usually happy to make adjustments in their own way of life to provide for their children.

However, there is another cost: the income parents could have had but which they (usually the mother) sacrifice when they have children because they are then less able to take paid work. This 'opportunity cost' is a new influence on parents in their decisions about having children – new because the two-income-earner pattern of family life is new and because the expectation of having two incomes is new. This is the influence which determines whether (potential) parents feel that they can afford to have children and then take on the direct costs. If parents find that the opportunity cost is too high, they may hesitate with having children. If they have children not knowing the opportunity cost, they may find it difficult to provide properly for them.

The opportunity cost for parents today is high – up to a third of potential income for young families with young children – and it is rising. This is contributing to reluctance in family formation, low birth rates and child poverty.

1. The opportunity cost of raising children should be compensated to parents through a universal child allowance with a level and distribution to make child rearing affordable and to encourage higher birth rates.
2. The child allowance should be approximately 20 per cent of average family disposable income for each child for the first five years and then gradually reduced up to the age of, say, fifteen.
3. The child allowance should be paid to the mother and be taxable income on top of other family income.

3. Family decisions

It is a principle of liberal ethics that citizens should not have decisions imposed upon them without their own participation. Participation is necessary for fairness and for the purpose of deliberation so as to increase the chances of cooperation in finding sensible solutions to difficult problems. The values of fairness and deliberation are protected in institutions which award members equal rights and impose on them equal duties. For families to have this capacity, they need a firm basis in marriage or family contract.

In some respects, families have been strengthened as institutions of joint decision making, for example between husband and wife in matters of property. Children's rights are increasingly recognised. In other respects, the family institution has been weakened. Through the acceptance of informal cohabitation, decision making on family formation has been effectively deregulated. The availability of cohabitation encourages unions of weak commitment. Divorce and abortion are increasingly subject to individual decision making. In these matters the libertarian principle of unfettered individualism has crowded out the more demanding and difficult liberal ethic of equal say and joint decision making.

1. Formal marriage should be encouraged and informal cohabitation discouraged. If society is neutral on cohabitation versus marriage, the likelihood is that cohabitation advances over marriage. New unions of weak commitment are encouraged.
2. Divorce and abortion have become too easily available. In these decisions, procedures of more explicit deliberation should be introduced to safeguard fair say and participation for both parties, and possibly for children. The individualisation of important family decisions weakens the notion of the family as an institution of equal rights and duties.

4. Children and voting

In democratic politics, politicians pay attention to the interests of voters and offer them policies which are in their interest so as to attract their votes. This is the way democracy is supposed to work and this is how it does work (albeit imperfectly). Children are not voters.

Politicians therefore pay less attention to the interests of children than to the interests of other citizens, in particular large groups of voters who are likely to turn out at election time, such as the elderly. Politicians do this not out of cynicism or ill will but because they must listen to voters in order to survive the next election. As a result, the interests of children – which are also interests that lie in the long-term development of society – are poorly represented in political decision making. Children (and long-term interests) lose out in the democratic struggle over attention and government policies. In Britain, for example, children have carried a disproportionate share of the burden of redistribution during the recent years of rising inequality.

1. The interests of children should be given representation in the franchise. Since children cannot vote, a new flexibility is needed in the organisation of voting.
2. The age of voting should be reduced to, say, sixteen. The votes of younger children should be exercised on their behalf by custodians.
3. Mothers should administer two votes, their own and one for their young children which they exercise separately and on their behalf.

Family revolution

For centuries, European populations have lived their lives in families – not extended families, not kinship families, but families as we know them in modern times. Today, this age-old institution is under pressure from changing patterns of family life, falling birth rates, new divisions of labour between family, market and government in work, production and child rearing, and changing values. These changes are rapid and far-reaching, with consequences for families, the living conditions of children and economic and social life as a whole. So profound is the pressure on the family and its role in society that I believe it is correct to use the term 'revolution'.

We are far from having a full understanding of how the family is changing or what the causes and consequences are. But some themes emerge from both public debate and research.

One theme is the evolution of freedoms of various kinds. Research on social attitudes suggests a growing sense of 'self-realisation' as a value and of the right to put self before social obligations. There is increasing acceptance of new forms of family life: cohabitation, children outside of marriage, single parenthood, divorce. There are more opportunities for married women (with children) to work outside of the family and to participate in social and political life. More of the young appear to be choosing non-family as a lifestyle and to be deciding against having children.

Another theme is awareness of what families in fact do. They 'produce' children and raise the next generation of citizens. Family life gives order and discipline to work and community participation. Families educate the young and pass on to them identity, values and norms, social and practical skills, and an understanding of rights and wrongs. They provide their members with material consumption and with 'services' such as childcare and care for others, the old and the ill. And they are the setting for intimate and emotional life.

If the family is to be efficient in what it does, it needs a solid basis of organisation, resources and commitment, as do all institutions for efficiency. If family members increasingly believe that self-realisation is to be found outside of family life, some of the basis for family efficiency may crumble. If the family becomes less efficient, we become more dependent on other arrangements and institutions for what families cannot manage: more dependent on the money economy for material consumption, more dependent on schools and pre-schooling for identity, values and the training of citizenship, more dependent on government for care and services.

The pressures on the family are not only from changing values and attitudes; there are also changes in harder realities. In thinking about family formation, young people consider what they think is expected of them in strongly competitive labour markets. In deciding on having children, parents ask themselves if they can afford to. In deciding on family work and paid work, we look to what income we need to pay for housing, transport, childcare and other demands. If some are giving family less priority, they may feel they can do so because the welfare state provides support and services. Young people can see that families are not stable and may have good reasons to fear that family is a high-risk strategy for their lives. Thus, the family revolution, predictably, is tied up in a web of economic and social change, of welfare state organisation, and of both rationality and folly in the way people are able to arrange their lives.

Politicians, commentators and the public are aware of the pressures on the family, as seen in press and media debate, government planning documents and elsewhere. But for all our concern with 'family values', it is still difficult to recognise the force of family change.

First, our perceptions are distorted by some mistaken beliefs in history. It is widely held that in Europe the industrial revolution also brought about family revolution, from extended families to nuclear families. This belief leads us to see the family as a historical peculiarity which belongs to the period of industrialism and which should be expected to fade as we move towards post-industrialism. However, we now know from research in historical demography that the nuclear family household as the norm is much older than the period of industrialism. It is now, towards the end of the twentieth century, that we have family revolution – away from the nuclear family and towards who knows what? As always, those who live through revolution fail to recognise it because even during revolution one day is much like the other.

Second, our perception is distorted by some mistaken beliefs about modern society. In the social sciences, the dominant theory of modernisation is that institutions increasingly specialise and that modern societies are characterised by strict divisions of labour between institutions. The family, it is believed, specialises in 'being social' and in the satisfaction of emotional needs. It then follows that if social and emotional needs can be met outside the family setting, not much is lost to society if the family weakens. Whatever merit the general theory may have, the suggestion that families are just for social and emotional needs is a grave misrepresentation of what modern families in fact do. A firm conclusion from recent research on family life is that families do much more than 'being social'.

Third, our perspective is distorted by shortcomings in the way we measure economic and social progress and, hence, in what we are being told, on expert authority, about how well off we are. Standard methods for the measurement of economic progress exaggerate the value of production, which can be measured in money, and underestimate the value of production outside the money economy, in particular in the family economy. While there are robust methods of economic accounting, the technology of social accounting is less developed: Therefore we are often more guided by economic indicators for society than by social indicators of how people live.

I have made this comparison elsewhere. The late nineteenth century had to deal with the 'worker question': how to reorganise social and political relations in response to the emerging working class so as to preserve legitimacy and cohesion in society. It took 50 years of analysis to understand the problem and another 50 years to put in place the welfare state. The late twentieth century has to deal with the 'family question'. Are we now, both individually and as a society, less able to turn to the family for our needs than European population has been used to? If so, how are we to live our intimate lives, from where are we to have identity, how are we to raise children, how are we to pass on values and educate citizens, from where are we to get social stability and guidance? Is the analysis going to take us equally long, and what are we to do? Will future historians ask, 'Why did they not see? Why was nothing done?'

How much is the family worth?

What do families do? A great deal, obviously. In families, people live their daily lives, they have children and raise them, they seek to satisfy their emotional needs, they provide each other with support and a foothold for activities outside of the family, and more. Family life is a source of identity and of security. It is where we learn values and norms and about right and wrong. The experience of family gives the individual guidance and a sense purpose and direction in work and citizenship, and is how new members of the human tribe acquire social skills. The family is not the only institution in society which serves these purposes, but it is basic to them. Not all families function well or equally well, and there are downright bad families in which life is a nightmare. But there would not be families, and we would not for centuries have lived our lives in families, unless those who form families saw them as being useful to their lives.

I think it is not in question that the family provides emotional care and that it is a site of social life, and there is no need to provide proof of this. But many do believe that the family has been removed from the economy and that it has become 'only social'. Family members leave the family for jobs in the economy, where they produce things and earn an income, enabling them to earn money, which they use to buy goods in the market, which they take back to the family for consumption. This we do, but we do more in the family than this sketch suggests. It is the mistaken belief of a division of labour between family and economy which causes us to underestimate what is done in the family.

I here draw attention to the economics of the family. I do this not because I believe economy is the most important thing in the family;

I actually believe it is the least important side of family life and is nothing but the resource base for what is of true importance. I look to the economy because we know that the family is social, because some say it is only social and because proof that it is also economic is thus proof that it is more important than the theorists of modernisation will have it.

I will discuss below no-nonsense material consumption standard of living and nothing else. I am not moving into any kind of 'soft' expanded concept of quality of life. For example, I will be considering family production but will include in that only household work proper and not childcare or other care activities. I am being as dogmatically economic as the most single-minded economist could wish to be. I am not using a new or redefined concept of economics, I am saying only that economics do not stop at the family door.

Value added

When a family sits down to a meal, family members enjoy the end product of a range of activities in the market as well as the household. Activities in the market include farming and fishing, processing, packaging, storage and transportation, through to the ready goods in supermarkets. Activities by the family include shopping, the preparation and cooking of the food, the setting of the table and afterwards the washing up. In all these activities, whether in the market or the family, labour power and capital go into the production: the farmer's time and the use of his tractor, the wife's or husband's time and the use of tools, stoves and dishwashers. Families could have their meals without any work of their own if they went to restaurants, but much of the time we make our own meals (for good economic reasons).[1]

Once we start to look, we find a great deal of production by families themselves, such as the production of meals and a clean dwelling (unless we pay a housekeeper), the production of clean clothes (unless we take them to a laundry), and the maintenance of house, car, equipment, clothing and garden (unless we pay a caretaker).[2] These activities are so obvious to us in our daily affairs that we may find it difficult or artificial to think of them as economic activities. But all these ordinary family activities are in fact production, every bit as much as when similar activities are provided in the market for pay.

If we look more closely, we find something else that is even more difficult to notice because it is even more obvious. Family members cooperate: they cooperate in producing things, as we do in market work, and they cooperate in consumption. Family cooperation is, as is well known, not always harmonious but without cooperation a family would not be a family. Cooperation in consumption consists in the shared use of common goods. If a single person lives in a house, he has housing from that house. If a second person moves in, she will also have housing from the same house without the first person having to give up his housing. As if by magic, through cooperation two persons (or more) can both (or all) have housing from one house (although sooner or later, if the family grows, it will need a larger house). Similarly for the use of tools, equipment, TV sets, cars and the like.

We do not live family lives for the purpose of economising in consumption, or not only for that purpose, but that is nevertheless a reality of what families do. In family cooperation, there are economies of scale which enable us together to get more consumption out of our income than we could have had if we had all lived alone.

A family has a certain income (which may come from work, capital or government transfers). With this income it can buy goods in the market.[3] If we know the family's income, we know what it has or can have of market goods. But we do not know the standard of living of the members of the family. Market goods are really only raw materials which are processed further in the family before they reach family members as consumption. Two things are added by the family itself. First, it adds production: the family adds goods of its own making to the goods it buys in the market. Second, it adds cooperation: through economies of scale family members get more consumption out of the available goods than if they just shared out the goods without further cooperation in their use. If we wish to know the real standard of living of the members of this family, we must look to their consumption after family production and cooperation.[4]

This real standard of living, including value added in the family, can be estimated. Family income is a measure of market goods available to the family. Family production can be estimated from the production value of the time family members invest in household work. When this value is added to family income, we have the total value of goods available to the family from the market and its own work. The value of cooperation can be estimated with the help of conventional techniques to account for economies of scale. From that, we can convert the value of goods available to the family to the value of consumption available to each family member. Appendix A gives a summary of some such estimates for Britain.

In estimates of this kind, there is uncertainty because we do not have enough precise knowledge about family economics and because our techniques and data are not perfect. The procedure used presently is based on prudent assumptions which deliberately keep estimates low so as to assure that the element of uncertainty errs in the direction of caution.[5] This is the value of family production and cooperation in Britain (see Appendix A):

1. Through their own production, families on average add between 50 and 60 per cent to the value of the goods available to them from the market through money income.
2. On top of the sum of market goods and goods produced in the family, another third is added through cooperation.
3. Taken together, family production and cooperation increase the value of consumption to household members by well over 100 per cent compared to the per capita value of money income. This, obviously, does not mean that we could dispense with income, because without market goods for raw materials families could do nothing. But it does mean that our material standard of living would have been less than half of what it in fact is if it were not for family production and cooperation.

This result, based on conservative assumptions which deliberately hold estimates down, is in my view an astonishing one for an advanced economy, in which the family is often believed to have become economically marginal. It is a result which totally destroys the theory that the family has been removed from the economy and that there is a division of labour between the 'social' family and the 'economic' market.

If we define the national economy as those processes which create material consumption, we can say conservatively that half of the nation's economy exists inside the nation's families.

Trends

Patterns of economic activity change over time. In modern economies, although the family remains a potent economic institution we do see a reduction of economic activity in the family in favour of market production. We buy more ready-made food, we are more inclined to pay professionals to do maintenance work than to do it ourselves, we buy new things instead of repairing old ones.

While there is growth in the market economy, there is decline in the family economy. Since our standard of living depends on both, in about equal measure, we need to consider both trends in order to assess correctly how well off we are and whether our standard of living is improving. Since the trends are not the same in family production and market production, income measures, which observe only the market economy, do not tell us how well off we are or how our standard of living is developing.

Take it as a thought experiment that all persons in a population live on their own (no family cooperation) and add nothing to the goods they can buy in the market (no family production). What would their standard of living be? This we know: it would be, on average, income per person; it would be what we believe it to be by ordinary per capita income measures of economic standards and growth. However, that is not the way we live. There are families and in families there is production and cooperation through which value is added on top of market goods. The trends are not the same in family production and market production. Therefore, income measures, which observe only the market economy, do not tell us how well off we are and how this is developing.

There is a long distance between goods from the market and consumption by persons. First, the available goods must be distributed to families. In Britain during the past twenty years, there has been a massive redistribution of income towards inequality. Although there are additional goods in the market, the majority of families have had less than the equivalent additional purchasing power. Income for families with children, for example, has increased less than the overall income growth in the population.

Second, to secure a reasonable income, many families have had to increase their work effort, in particular they have become dependent on two jobs. The price is increasing stress and strain.

Third, modern families are becoming less productive in their own economic activities. They have become smaller: fewer children, more single persons living on their own, more lone parents. This is costly. With smaller families, the population will need more of those things that are shared by families, such as houses, cars, TV sets, equipment, in order to provide all persons with housing, transport, leisure and other forms of consumption. We need more goods simply to prevent the standard of living from declining. Family behaviour is changing: with more time in paid work, there is less time for household work. When less is done in the family, more must be bought in the market. Even if the consumption we get were the same, more of it would come out of cash income and less from the family's own production.

Income measures of economic growth have a built-in error since they consider only half of the economy. When production shifts from the family to the market, it also shifts from being 'hidden' to becoming measured. Some of what looks to be economic growth in the income statistics is not growth at all: it is only the same production shifted into the sphere where the statisticians happen to have their instruments of measurement.

Between 1976 and 1986, economic growth in Britain as measured by income was 31 per cent (see Appendix A). The standard of living, however, measured after family production and cooperation, increased by only 23 per cent. Between a third and a quarter of market economic growth was absorbed by less value added in families before it reached persons for consumption. That does not include the error in the measurement of growth resulting from production shifting out of the family and into the market. This magnitude is not known, but if what is not produced in the family is about a third of the growth measure, it would be a reasonable assumption that about the same were shifted into the market, in which case there would be no more than about 10 or 15 per cent left of growth in real standard of living behind the 31 per cent estimate. And that is before we have accounted for increasing stress and effort and rising inequality. Hence, even with reasonable economic growth in the market economy, there is not much improvement in most people's standard of living.

Discussion

Social scientists in many countries have observed a 'paradox of afflu-ence': people wish to have a higher standard of living but when they get it they find themselves no more satisfied. Politicians are bewildered about the 'feelgood factor' (as it is known in Britain), or rather its absence, and about the 'joyless recovery' (as it is known in the United States). The statistics tell them that there is economic growth but their constituents tell them that they do not feel better off.

There are two possible explanations of this paradox. One is that people are confused about how they wish to live their lives: they believe they wish to have a higher level of consumption, but they subsequently find that that is doing them no good. The problem with this explanation is that it assumes that people have no sense of what is in their own best interest. One would think that if we realised that there was no real value to us in more consumption, we would move to other priorities. In fact, people are not fanatical about material consumption and do not confuse the use and ownership of things with the good life, but we do continue to want an increase in our mate-rial standard.

The other explanation is more simple: there is no paradox; the reason people do not feel better off is that they are not better off. The confusion lies not in the way people understand and think about their lives, but in the way economists and statisticians measure standards of living and economic growth and the information citizens and politi-cians are getting from these statistics.

It may be useful for many purposes to have measures of the volume of goods produced in the market and how this changes. Income measures tell us this and that is excellent in its own right. The problem, however, is that these measures tend to be seen as telling us what our *standard of living* is and whether or not we are getting better off. In fact, they do not tell us this, but that is how they are interpreted. Because we have no authoritative measures of the real standard of living, we there-fore look to what we do have for want of anything better. People are not confused about their lives; we should never trust explanations which assume that people do not know what is in their own best interest. The confusion is in what they are being told, on expert authority, about how the material conditions of their lives are evolving.

How much do children cost?

It is a remarkable fact of modern life that we can choose whether or not to have children. Never before in human experience has this been a choice. Not having children is perhaps not a realistic collective choice, but it is a real choice for each person or couple. Birth control techniques are easily available, because of social security we do not need children of our own to support us in old age and it is socially acceptable to be childless. This gives a dramatic importance to family economics: if child rearing is expensive it will be discouraged, if it is affordable it will be encouraged.

The presence of children can influence the economic situation of families in two ways, on costs and on income. It is costly to raise children. They need housing, food, clothing, equipment, toys, school material, transportation and many other things. Although such costs are high, and growing, they are not a major concern for parents. Parents are aware of these costs, are prepared to accept outlays for the benefit of their children and are usually prepared to make adjustments in their own standard of living if that is needed. This they do – if they can afford it. For parents, the concern is not cost but affordability. The first question in the economics of child rearing is whether parents can both have children and earn a sufficient income to support them.

Having children may exert two entirely different influences on family income. There may be an encouragement effect: the needs of children represent a pressure on parents to earn more income. And there may be a discouragement effect: parents need to devote time and attention to their children and have less freedom of manoeuvre in the labour market. For working mothers, having children strongly influences their labour market activity. They withdraw from the labour market, for a shorter or longer period, and if they return to paid work, which may well then be part-time, the absence may represent a handicap in their career prospects. The result is a loss of income, both the immediate effect resulting from work absence and a long-term career effect. For working fathers, children are of less consequence. Most fathers continue their work pretty much as they have, although there is some evidence to suggest that having children encourages fathers to earn more income than they otherwise might have. These patterns obviously reflect gender divisions of labour in family and paid work which may change, although they seem to be remarkably entrenched.

Opportunity cost

It is clear enough today that the discouragement effect (carried by mothers) is stronger than the encouragement effect (carried by fathers, if there is one). Overall, families sacrifice income by having children. This is true for annual income – which is the most relevant issue of concern in respect to the affordability of having children – and to lifetime income. The reasons are that mothers now tend to have and to wish to have paid work, that the earnings of women are therefore more important for family income and that family income becomes more 'sensitive' to children since female earnings are more 'sensitive' to children. Under more traditional family arrangements with the single male breadwinner and married women staying at home, the influence of children on family income was much weaker.

Since families sacrifice income by having children, we can say that they face an 'opportunity cost' of children. When they have children, they give up income they would have had the opportunity to earn had they not had children. It is possible to estimate the opportunity cost. A sample of such estimates is given in Appendix B.

Obviously, we cannot know what income people would have earned had they lived a different life from the life they actually live. Nor can we know what income families would have had in a society with drastically more or drastically fewer children; that would have been a society with different life-forms. But we can know this: we can observe what families earn, we can observe what families with children and families without children earn, and we can thus observe the earnings of families which are similar to one another except for the difference that some have children and others not. That difference we can take as reflecting the influence of children on family income or, in other words, how parents must expect their income to be affected by having children.[6] For British families it works out like this (see Appendix B):

1. As a general rule, families do indeed sacrifice income when they have children. This is universally the case for young families and it is universally the case for families with young children.[7]
2. The first child has the greatest impact on income. Young families (head of household under 30) with a single child under five sacrifice up to a third of their potential income. The momentous decision, as far as income goes, is the decision to move from not having children to having children.
3. After the first child, there is an additional, although modest, income sacrifice following additional children.
4. As families and children grow older, the income sacrifice goes down. For example, for families in the age group 30 to 39 (head of household) who have a single child under five, the income sacrifice is about 20 per cent (as compared to about 30 per cent in the younger age group). In the same age group of families, with a single child between five and nine, the income sacrifice is short of 10 per cent.
5. Over time, the opportunity cost of children has increased, over the ten year period of observation, from between 22 and 27 per cent to around 30 to 37 per cent for young families with the youngest child under five.

Affordability of children

It is an absolute certainty – now that we can choose not to have children – that we will not have children unless we can afford them. We wish to have children, we wish to maintain the family line, we wish our population to prosper; in this nothing has changed. But we are no longer doomed by necessity to follow this wish; in this everything has changed. Wishing something is not enough; we cannot have what we wish unless we can afford it. If children are unaffordable, and we can choose, we will either have none or we will have as few as we can.

In one sense, we can today afford children better than previously since we are more affluent. But affordability is more subjective than this. When the standard of living increases, so do our expectations and our understanding of what is a necessary standard. We have more money, more goods, and more consumption (although not as much as we sometimes think), but we do not have, or at least we do not feel that we have, more disposable money. Our income is permanently tied up in needs which follow previous decisions – home, car, mortgage – and which impose themselves on us by what the society around us takes to be necessities.

Equally important is the way families organise themselves for the attainment of what they see as a necessary standard of living. Today, the two-earner family is the norm. Families feel that they need two incomes to have a satisfactory standard of living, and gainful employment for mothers and married women is seen as desirable for other reasons. Previously, most families, at least families with children, were single-earner families. The wife, if she was in gainful employment before marriage, would usually leave work on marrying and certainly would expect to do so when the time came for children. This family had a lower standard of living than the average family today, but the question of the affordability of children did not present itself as it does today since there was virtually no opportunity cost. There was no income earned by the wife that had to be sacrificed. There was still the cost of supporting children, but then as now this is not what parents worry about.

The modern family is more affluent but it is also more economically vulnerable. It depends for its standard of living on two incomes. When it has children, one of those incomes must be given up, fully or in part, for a shorter or longer period – hence the opportunity cost, hence the question of affordability. That question, which now poses itself with strength to young people forming families and to prospective parents, is as new a question as is the remarkable fact that we can choose whether or not to have children. In the course of two or three generations, the economic circumstances around decisions about child rearing have been totally redefined. Paradoxically, although we are more affluent, children have become less affordable.

Family support

Europe is undergoing a serious population crisis. Birth rates are too low for the reproduction of the population, and they are too low for the preservation of economic vitality.[8] To attain adequate birth rates, child rearing must be made affordable. We organise one part of our social life – work and family – so as to make ourselves more dependent on cash income jobs. This brings upon us a new problem of children becoming less affordable. If we want children, or more children, we must make child rearing more affordable. It is not certain that affordability will be enough to increase or maintain birth rates, since there are many other factors which influence parents' decisions about having children, but it is certain that without affordability it will not happen.

Since there is no way back to the one-earner family – never mind the question of whether or not that would be desirable – the opportunity cost must be eliminated through family support. The reorganisation of social life has imposed a new cost of raising children on to parents. This cost should be carried by society and not left to parents. Society should take that cost on out of fairness and out of necessity. It is in the interest of the whole population that the population is reproduced and that families can provide adequately for children. Those who do not have children have an economic advantage which it is reasonable that they share. Young people will turn away from child rearing if it is not affordable.[9]

How should families with children be supported? One possibility is through provisions specifically for families with working mothers, such as childcare facilities, so as to make the combination of child rearing and work easier. The other possibility is through a universal child allowance to all parents on a level adequate to compensate for the opportunity cost. The former would work for two income families and for families in which both parents wish to work, but not for parents who are less able to work (for example single mothers) or who do not both wish to work. The latter would work for all families and would make it possible for parents themselves to decide how they wish to balance family and paid work. For liberals, the free choice argument must always weight heavily. This suggests a policy which benefits all families equally, irrespective of life style, and goes against a policy which is to the benefit of certain life styles above others.

How might a child allowance look if it were to be adequate to compensate for the opportunity cost? That cost is highest for the youngest families, at about 30 per cent. Should that be compensated? Early entry into child rearing should probably not be encouraged. Modern economies are becoming more and more education dependent, and equality of opportunity depends increasingly on education. Early entry into child rearing would interfere with educational opportunities, in particular for women.

The opportunity cost is highest at the point of entry into child rearing, that is, with the first child. There is an additional (modest) opportunity cost for additional children. The opportunity cost argument would therefore suggest a high child allowance for the first child, a lower allowance for additional children, and a gradual reduction of the child allowance as children grow older. Child allowance for a duration of, say, fifteen years for each child would seem adequate.

However, there is also a birth rate argument. If we believe birth rates are too low, which they are, it is not enough to encourage people to have children, it is necessary to also encourage the third and fourth child.

Taken together, these arguments suggest a child allowance at a level equivalent to 20 per cent of average family disposable income for each child the first five years, and then gradually reduced up to the age of about fifteen, when it would be terminated.

It is known from research that mothers are more likely that fathers to spend income under their control for the benefit of their children. The child allowance should therefore be paid to the mother.

A problem with a universal child allowance it that it also benefits parents who are on a high enough income level so that they do not need child support (although this is a small proportion of families with small children) and that, because of progressive taxation, it may be relatively worth more to high income families than to low income families. The policy might for these reasons be seen as unfair and lose support in public opinion (as has happened in Britain). The child allowance should therefore be taxable income on top of other family income.

Family decisions:
divorce and abortion

I propose an experiment: consider the family to be a society of citizens and apply to this little society the elementary rules of democracy.

At the core of democratic principle, and of liberal ethics, is the simple idea that citizens have a right of equal say in those decisions which are important to them and that they have a right to not have decisions imposed upon them. They do not have a right, obviously, to always have their way in decisions, since others have equally valid interests, but they have a right to have their say and to have their views and interests respected equally with those of others.

This principle is not a given. One can disagree with it. One can believe that society is so complicated that only those with exceptional competence should be allowed to take part in decision making. This, it seems to me, is the stronger idea in the history of political philosophy. Or one can believe that the individual has an absolute right to decide as he or she wishes and that no one else has a right to impose their interests on him or her. This, it seems to me, is the libertarian ideology which has so many followers today.

One can disagree with this idea, and many have and many do, but one cannot, I believe, disagree with it and still be a liberal. Liberals believe that everyone has a right to have their interests respected and that we therefore have a duty to respect the interests of others.

Family decisions
There are two tenets behind the liberal principle of participation. The first is fairness. If all are equal as citizens, it follows that everyone should have a say in important decisions. The second is good decision

making. If we assure deliberation so that decisions are not made until all views are heard and all interests considered, the chances are good that we will be able to find suitable and acceptable solutions to difficult problems.

The implication for decision making procedures is to regulate institutions so that they follow rules of fairness, deliberation, transparency and the like. Thus, we impose on businesses, for example, rules of contract and accountability, and on political institutions, such as Parliament, rules of committee preparation and of multiple readings of prospective bills of law. Such rules are intended to make decision procedures cumbersome so as to discourage the danger of decisions which are unfair or which lack reason.

The current state of family law is confusing and ambiguous. One trend is towards stricter rules of fairness and deliberation in family decisions, whereby the rights of women, and to some degree of children, have been strengthened. For example, husbands are no longer able to make decisions about joint property without the consent of wives. Another trend is towards the removal of rules around family formation. While until recently families were formed through marriage, informal cohabitation is now increasingly accepted and practised and the marriage contract is coming to be seen as less of a binding commitment. A third trend is the individualisation of some family decisions and the removal or weakening, in these decisions, of safeguards of fairness and deliberation. This applies, in particular, to divorce and abortion.

This ambiguity about family decisions is a reflection of the general confusion about the modern family. If we see the family as mainly an emotional community, it might seem reasonable that it should be free from regulation. But if the family is an institution of production and decision making, it would be reasonable to see it, like any other institution, as in need of regulation for fairness and efficiency.

The family is both of these, but as I have tried to argue in the preceding chapters, the importance of the modern family as an institution of production is gravely underestimated. If it is right that this aspect of the family institution should be emphasised more strongly, a concern would follow for rules around family formation and family decision making. That, in turn, would necessarily bring us to the question of family or marriage contract. It is not possible to assure fairness in the decisions of an institution unless it is firmly established as such. For example, property in marriage is subject to joint decision making in force of the marriage contract. If a couple live together without contract, the weaker party has little or no protection for fairness if they come into conflict.[10] In families, no less than in other institutions, it is difficult to assure fairness and rationality in internal affairs unless there are explicit rules about rights, duties and procedure of decision making – it is not enough to hope for the best.

I do not consider here procedures around family formation, except for some comments on cohabitation towards the end of the chapter. Instead, I start from the assumption that a family contract exists and then ask what follows for family decisions when the liberal principle of participation is applied to them. To sharpen the experiment, I put under the microscope those most difficult of family questions, divorce and abortion, which are being individualised in current family law.

Social contract

I take as my point of departure four principles of democratic procedure. First, a democratic society is based on a social contract about rights and duties. All those included in the contract are citizens with equal rights and duties. Second, the basic right is the right to free and equal participation in the making of decisions in which one has an interest. Third, the basic duty is to accept and comply, in good faith, with decisions which are made through proper democratic process. Fourth, rights and duties are tempered by due concern for others and hence are not absolute. We cannot without compromise exercise freedoms which infringe on the freedom of others, and there are minority rights.

A family, in my meaning, rests on a contract by which a couple have committed themselves to each other, and possibly agreed to have children, whether the contract is formalised or informal.[11] The citizens in this society are the man and the woman and the children who live with them. I do not consider involuntary arrangements, for example forced marriage or pregnancy as a result of rape. In these circumstances, a family in my meaning does not exist and nothing of what I say here applies (although I recognise that the dividing lines between agreed and forced marriage and consent and rape may not always be easy to draw).[12]

An existing social contract may break down. In a large society, this could be the result of a coup d'état; in a family, it could be the result of, for example, infidelity. In contract theory, it is recognised that serious grievance is needed for an existing contract to be declared null and void, since otherwise a contract would not be a contract. The American Declaration of Independence, for example, which is precisely about a social contract which has broken down, underlines strongly the need for serious and valid complaint to justify exit (and then gives a long list of such complaints against George III).

Under what circumstances a family contract would be considered to have broken down is not easy to determine. With infidelity, for example, one would hardly say that the sinner is released from her or his duties (although possibly the sinned against is) or that parents have fewer commitments to their children. Certainly, a contract does not break down by one partner unilaterally deciding to opt out. A marriage contract, for example, would not be a contract if the presumption were that it stands only as long as there is agreement to continue it. Irretrievable breakdown is a reality, but it would not make sense to say that there is irretrievable breakdown whenever one partner declares there to be irretrievable breakdown. Persons who have freely entered into a contract have a right of exit only when exit can be justified explicitly and on the basis of serious and valid grievance (or, obviously, if others release them from their commitment).

These are difficult questions which I do not propose to resolve here. I only wish to stress, although it is perhaps obvious, that once a contract has been entered into freely by responsible persons, it becomes a binding commitment. I assume a family in my contractual understanding and the questions of divorce or abortion that may arise in such a family.

Divorce

By divorce, I mean a decision to end the commitment that partners have previously made to each other.[13] Those who have an interest in this decision are the partners and their children if they have any.

The simplest case is a couple without children who both agree to end their union. Divorce is a fair and just decision. Now assume that the one wants divorce and the other wants the union to continue. If the preferences of both are to count equally, there is a deadlock. In democratic procedure, there are two possible solutions to deadlock. One is that someone is given a casting vote, for example the chairman of a committee, and the other is to continue the process until the deadlock is broken by persuasion.

In the case of the disagreeing couple, there is no basis for assigning a casting vote to either one of the two since that would disqualify the other. Neither of the two has any claim to *a priori* superior authority; there is no 'chairman' in a marriage (or at least there should not be). Allocating a casting vote is in itself a decision and it must be legitimate, for example based on the understanding that you have the casting vote today and I have it tomorrow. There is no legitimate way of resolving a deadlock between two persons with equal rights in a one-off decision with the help of a casting vote, since that would just be making the same decision in a different guise. Hence, on the basis of equal rights, the contract stands until there is agreement to end it.

A 'due concern' argument might apply if we were to say that one partner is more dependent than the other on the union and that therefore extra weight should be given to his or her preference. It is possible that the more dependent partner would be the one to insist on divorce, but one would normally expect the opposite. The introduction of due concern would, therefore, strengthen the view that the union continues until there is agreement to end it.

Current divorce law and practice in most countries give priority to the preference to end a union above the preference to continue it. Usually, some waiting period is prescribed, but if no consensus is reached at the end of this period, the divorce preference prevails. In fact, the partner who wants to end the union is given the casting vote. There are expediency reasons for so doing, but it is difficult to see how arguments of principle could support this. There exists a contract; why should the person who wants to maintain the contract be expected to be more ready to live with the unwanted decision than the person who wants to end the contract?

It might be argued that if a consensus cannot be reached even after a reasonable waiting time, then the marriage has broken down, but this is at odds with the principle of democracy which contains a duty to make the best of the best available solution even when that is not one's own preferred solution. No one has a right to undermine that principle by making life miserable for those who have a different position from one's own and thereby enforcing one's own will. In a union, both partners have the power to do this but a power is not a right. Of course, no one should have to live with someone they simply cannot stand, but this does not explain divorce. Many unions survive despite serious difficulties, indeed very few are without periods of serious difficulty, while others are allowed to collapse for trivial reasons.

Let us now bring children into the family, first one child. There are three citizens and possible majorities and minorities. If all agree on divorce, divorce is just. If there is a two-to-one majority, one way or the other, that majority view should normally prevail and it would be for the third person to make the best of it. For example, if the mother and the child (or the father and the child) agree that the union should continue, it would be for the father (or the mother) to comply. Again, it might be in his (or her) power to undermine the majority position, but a power is not a right.

Are there relevant due concern arguments or minority rights? Again, extra weight might be given to the most dependent, in particular to the opinion of the child. The child has come into the family by the parents' decision while they have entered family life by free will, and the child is more dependent and vulnerable. A child could obviously not enforce divorce against the will of parents, since parents also have rights, but there might be arguments to suggest that the child's opinion should have some priority if the child is against divorce, even if the parents agree that they want divorce. Again, the due concern argument pulls in the direction of preserving the union.

If there are two children, the same as above would apply in respect to majorities, minorities and due concern, but with some additions. Once again, there is the possibility of deadlock, two against two. If there is one parent and one child on either side, the position – as with the two disagreeing adults – cannot be resolved fairly by a casting vote since there is no reasonable argument for giving either side priority. If the vote were two adults against two children, there might be a due concern argument for giving the position of the children priority. If that were accepted, the two children in agreement would have a right of veto, even if the parents agreed that they wanted divorce.

If there are more than two children, there would be the possibility of a majority of children against the parents. Could parents claim minority rights? Intuitively, I would say that they could in the unlikely event that they had a majority of children against them insisting they divorce against their will, but not necessarily if they had a majority of children against them refusing a divorce the parents would otherwise have wanted. This is not abstract theory; no doubt many couples who would otherwise separate do stay together out of concern for their children (which, incidentally, is further evidence that divorce is not the result of breakdown but of decision).

Abortion

There is possibly a strong moral view that abortion is absolutely wrong and that there is no morally acceptable decision to be made. This may or may not be compatible with a view that abortion may be allowed if the pregnancy is life-threatening to the woman, but that is a decision which would then have to be made by medical expertise and would fall outside of the discussion I am pursuing here. I consider only the case where both parents are involved. If, for example, the man has abandoned the woman, he obviously has no say in the decision.

In his book *Life's Dominion*, Ronald Dworkin has suggested a 'paradigm liberal position' on abortion in four points.[14] First, abortion is morally problematic and is always a grave moral decision. Second, abortion is nevertheless morally justified for a variety of serious reasons which go beyond, for example, to save the woman's life. Third, a woman's concern for her own interests is an adequate justification for abortion under certain circumstances. Fourth, the decision on abortion rests ultimately with the woman who carries the foetus and the state has no business intervening, even to prevent morally impermissible abortions.

What agreement there would be among liberals on this paradigm is not easy to say (as Professor Dworkin recognises). The first three points are principles, the fourth concerns procedure. I would maintain that the first point is without question true and that this truth is of consequence. It is based on the notion that life is sacred and that abortion prevents life (whether or not life is taken). There is no right to abort, abortion is wrong except when specifically justified. The two next points are also true but not on moral grounds alone. (In the third principle, I would have preferred 'relevant justification' to 'adequate justification', for reasons which will become apparent.) They are true because they are necessary. These principles are not fully compatible with the first principle and do represent a compromise with the sacredness of life. However, without some compromise, there could be no other available moral position than that abortion is absolutely wrong and that is, empirically, an impossible position as we know from societies which try to suppress abortion. The attempt to uphold moral absolutes which are impossible is not acceptable in a liberal society because the result is hypocrisy and the temptation to use coercive means. In the case of abortion, a ban would drive the practice underground and seriously undermine social morality. This would be true even if a ban were introduced by majority decision. Considered and careful compromise with moral principles is morally right. Hence, the second and third points are true because necessary, but morally acceptable only given the first point.

The fourth point, however, which is about procedure, is problematic the moment we apply democratic principle. It might be useful to quote Dworkin in full:

'The fourth component in the liberal view is the political opinion . . . that at least until late in pregnancy, when the fetus is sufficiently developed to have interests of its own, the state has no business intervening even to prevent morally impermissible abortions, because the question of whether an abortion is justifiable is, ultimately, for the woman who carries the fetus to decide. Others – mate, family, friends, the public – may disapprove, and they may be right, morally, to do so. The law might, in some circumstances, oblige her to discuss her decision with others. But the state in the end must let her decide for herself; it must not impose other people's moral convictions upon her.'[15]

This, I believe, goes wrong for two reasons. First, it does not follow from the position that the state has no business to intervene, that it is the woman who must decide in the end. There are other interested parties, certainly the man, and if we are democrats, if we are liberals, we do not exclude interested parties. The state may not have a right to impose other people's moral convictions, but other persons who have a valid interest in the decision, such as fathers or potential fathers, are not 'other people' in this meaning.

Second, it does not follow from the position that, ultimately, the woman must decide, that the state has no business to intervene. State regulation of individual choice is not contrary to a liberal idea of individual freedom, at least as long as state regulation is decided democratically. State regulation does not mean that the state decides, it means that the state lays down rules for individuals within which they must confine their choices, which is obviously acceptable in respect to abortion following the first point in the liberal paradigm. I do not believe the state has a right to impose abortion decisions – on this I agree fully with Dworkin – but it can and should (and it does) prescribe how those decisions are to be made. This it should do so as to assure fair respect for the interests of all those affected.

Let me here insert a comment on freedom. The libertarian position is that we are free if no restrictions are imposed on choice, in particular by the state. The conservative position, going back to Burke, for example (which, after Isaiah Berlin,[16] is also the liberal position), is that we are free if we have the capability to exercise choice. That capability, I believe, is determined by basic liberties (which no one honourable disputes), by the individual's resources and the options he is offered in his environment (which are the components the liberal might stress) and by community, by which I mean social guidance for wisdom in choice (which is the component the conservative might stress). We human beings have the gift of reason but we have the capability to apply good judgement only when the conditions are right. Alone, we are helpless, not free.

There is a necessary tension in the non-libertarian concept of freedom whereby, in order to have the capability of exercising choice, we must accept some social discipline and relinquish absolute liberty in the libertarian sense. Sensible people know this. They therefore seek insurance in social arrangements which bind them to take advice and in which they have protection against the dangers of anarchic liberty. If we insist, as we should, that abortion is morally problematic, the decision on abortion is necessarily a difficult one. Those who face this decision should not be left alone and isolated with it, they should be able to benefit from community; they should have the insurance which comes with the restraining influence of community. That does mean infringement in unlimited liberty, but it also means protection against anomie. This, in itself, would not necessarily mean that it would not be for the woman to decide in the end, although it could mean that, but it certainly does bring 'others' into the process, possibly more strongly than Dworkin indicates.

The discussion about abortion is, I believe, often too much about state and individual and too little about individual and community. This is the libertarian fallacy: the mistaken idea that society consists of individuals and the state, and that the problem of freedom is defined by the relationship between state and individual. That is important, obviously, and if the state is repressive nothing else can rescue freedom. But it is not enough. We do not live as individuals in this way, we live as persons in interaction with family, friends, colleagues, neighbours; we live in community. We live as citizens; for the citizen there is between him and the state *democracy* in which he is a participant. Freedom rests on capability of action and of choice. That capability the state can take away but it cannot give. Freedom depends on the state, but also, and equally, on community.

How, then, to decide? There are two questions: Who are the interested parties? Are there due concern arguments that would give some interested parties a right of privilege?

The person at the centre of the matter is obviously the woman but she is not the only interested party. Is the foetus an interested party? If so, it has rights; if so, the right to life. We would be back to the absolute position that abortion is wrong and there would be no matter of procedure to consider. Dworkin argues that although life is sacred and abortion therefore morally problematic, a foetus (at least in the early part of the gestation) has and can have no interests and therefore no rights, and from this concludes that abortion can be morally justified. He also suggests, if I understand him correctly, that were we to accept that the foetus has interests and rights, there could be no moral justification for abortion. Rights, he suggests, arise from interests and interests from 'complex capacities', such as 'to enjoy or fail to enjoy, to form affections and emotions, to hope and expect, to suffer disappointment and frustration.'[17] Without such complex capacities, there are no interests and no rights. This does not undermine the principle that life is sacred and that abortion is morally problematic, but it rejects the argument that abortion is necessarily wrong because it violates the rights of the unborn child. The foetus does not have complex capacities, hence does not have interests and rights, hence abortion can be morally justified.

I do not find this attempt to 'prove' the possibility of morally justifiable abortion to be convincing. The concept of complex capacities is helpful and I accept and agree with the link to interests: there cannot be interests without capacities. I do not, however, agree that it from this follows, at least necessarily, that the foetus has no rights. First, it is an altogether common principle in moral and legal philosophy that rights exist beyond those who are present here and now. The whole constitutional tradition is to see the social contract as being between current, past and future generations. Second, many people may during the course of their lives find themselves, every bit as much as a foetus, without complex capacities, without for that reason having no rights. On this I would speak from a personal experience which Professor Dworkin's discussion has helped me to interpret. On the one occasion when I had a full anaesthetic, I woke up with a very strange feeling that I had for a period been without complex capacities, in fact without capacities at all, and that, in that state and during that period, I had no interests. I was glad to wake up, but my strange sensation was precisely that I during the period could not have had any interest in whether or not I did, since had I not woken up I could not have known. Therefore, I recognise very well the link between complex capacities and interests and this, I think, is a correct and profound observation.

I would, however, reject the further link from interests to rights. I would certainly insist that although I was for a period without complex capacities, I still had my full rights as a citizen. I would insist that it was my right to wake up again, that it was my doctors' duty to see to it that I did, to the best of their ability, and that the fact that for a time I had no interests, including in waking up, did not give these doctors, or anyone else, any right to decide over my life. My situation was, in respect to capacities, that of a foetus. I think it does not matter for the logic that I, contrary to the foetus, had had an earlier life period with complex capacities; during the period, I had not and could not have any awareness of this. Nothing that was done to me during the blackout could do any violence to the experiences I had already had; it could only affect, as for the foetus, my potential experiences.

I am inclined to believe that no philosophical proof is available for the moral justification of abortion. The task is to reconcile a practice of abortion, which is a necessity, with the moral principle that life is sacred, which is a truth. The way to do this, I think, is not by philosophical proof but by maintaining a constant awareness and a never-ending debate about abortion in which we insist on the sacredness of life and remind each other of the first part in the liberal agenda, to assure that we do not give in to the convenience and temptation to forget that abortion is always a grave moral decision. We have no way out other than to decide that abortion can be justified, and I believe that decision is morally justified on the argument of necessity, as long as this is firmly within the framework that abortion is morally problematic. Therefore, the foetus is not an interested party in a decision about abortion, because the position that it is an interested party impossible and untenable.

Is the man an interested party? Certainly, and there is no case at all to be made that the man should have no say. Therefore, *ceteris paribus,* the preferences of the woman and those of the man count equally. This brings us to exactly the same position as with divorce. If there is agreement between the two to abort, then abortion is just. It remains a grave moral decision but no one else is more suitable to make the difficult decision. This is the standard liberal position, except that the decision lies with the woman and the man jointly and with equal say, and not with the woman alone. If there is disagreement and deadlock, the pregnancy would go forward. There would be no justification for the man to pressure the woman to an abortion against her will or for the woman to insist on an abortion against the will of the man.

That is *ceteris paribus.* Are there due concern arguments which would lead us to accept a privileged right for one of the partners? It is widely accepted today that there are, that these arguments give the woman the privileged position and that the decision therefore in the end lies with the woman. The relevant argument is that the woman carries the foetus, or perhaps, more generally, motherhood. This is a strong position: it is compassionate, it is politically attractive and it is the only available position which could eliminate the problem of deadlock in the difficult issue of abortion; it is the position of the liberal instinct. However, it is not a position which stands up easily to scrutiny on principle.

What is it specifically in the fact that the woman carries the foetus that would give her the right to decide, when the pregnancy has been entered into by agreement? Is it because she carries the physical burden? That, however, was known at the outset and is a burden the man could not take on or share, even if he should be willing to or wish to. Carrying the foetus is not a duty imposed by others (except God or nature) in return for which these others might be expected to give up rights. Citizens should not be denied rights because of circumstances which are outside of their control. Is it because she is the mother and has the closeness to the foetus, and later to the child, that motherhood involves? If the argument is that motherhood (beyond pregnancy) is a burden, it is the same argument again. If it is that only the mother can 'understand', would it then not follow that motherhood is qualitatively different from fatherhood and that the whole notion of equal parental responsibility would fall? If motherhood is a good, would it then not follow that fathers are excluded and deprived, which could not possibly be an acceptable argument for further deprivation or discrimination?

So, is it, then, in the end for the woman to decide? Compassion seems to say yes, logic no. Perhaps it is better to follow compassion than logic? But is there not also a case of compassion for the man? At first, both wanted the child. Something happens. One changes his mind or her mind. Is it then more fair to the man to deny him fatherhood than it would have been to the woman had he tried to deny her motherhood by enforcing abortion against her will? In the end, the privileged position of the woman in respect of the decision on abortion, which without doubt is the position most liberals share, is possible, it seems to me, only at the cost of rejecting the principle of equal rights and therefore is, or should be, an unattractive position to the liberal. Even after considering possible due concern arguments, I believe abortion would only be the correct decision if there was agreement between the partners.

Are existing children in the family interested parties? They are. A new brother or sister is on the way and this is a matter of great importance to the children who are already in the family. The children may not know but that is of no consequence for the question of interests or rights. Those in power cannot deprive citizens of rights by withholding information. Once it is accepted that children have an interest in the matter, the arguments are, in principle, the same as with divorce. Children could not enforce abortion against the will of agreeing parents but, albeit unlikely in practice, in theory could tip the balance if the parents disagree and possibly veto abortion against the will of agreeing parents.

Conclusion

Some findings follow from this experiment in the linking of family and democracy. First, if families are societies based on social contract with equal rights and duties, original agreements – to live together, to have a child – stand unless there is new agreement to the contrary, or at least majority agreement with due concern to minority interests. Second, once there are children in the family, the nature of the decision on divorce as well as the decision on abortion changes. It becomes more difficult to reach consensus, and divorce and abortion become less available to the parents. With more children, it is all the more difficult. This is entirely as it should be. Overall, decisions about divorce and abortion should not be treated as individual decisions. They are, and should be, joint decisions.

Democracy in institutions means joint decision making: all who have a valid interest in a matter have a say in its resolution. When joint decision making is desired, institutions need to be regulated to assure fair procedure. In current family law, some decisions have come under regulation for fairness, for example decisions about property, while other decisions have been increasingly deregulated, such as divorce and abortion. The price for deregulation is less emphasis on fairness and deliberation in family decision making. Rather than individualising family decisions, we should strengthen the notion that families are based on a contract of mutually recognised rights and duties and thereby reduce the danger of decisions which are unfair or lack reason.

We liberals have a firm opinion about how decisions should be made: with equal say. We sometimes also have opinions about what the right decisions are. On some social questions, the liberal instinct goes further towards individualism than it should on the basis of liberal opinion about how decisions are to be made. We allocate casting votes and then side with those who are thus given the power to enforce their will, with power over persuasion, with expediency over fairness. We come to side with opinion which is more libertarian than it is liberal. We wish to be liberal but the liberal position is not an easy one. We let ourselves be tempted by an easier position and make ourselves libertarians in disguise.

Postscript: cohabitation

Informal cohabitation has become more common and formal marriage less common. Is cohabitation a sensible alternative to marriage?

Formal marriage and informal cohabitation are different things, they are not the same thing in two different forms. Marriages are more durable than cohabitations, are based on more explicit commitments, and are protected by the institution of a formal contract. Marriages have a stronger effect than cohabitations of providing discipline and lifestyle guidance to the partners.

If one believes when entering into a union that it is probably not going to last, one has good reasons to cohabit and not to marry. If one believes that one is entering a union which one wishes to last, one has good reasons to marry and not cohabit. Everyone knows that unions come into difficulty. If one wishes to protect the union against the danger of collapsing in the face of difficulty which one knows will arise, one has reason to bind oneself in advance so as to make exit difficult and to protect oneself against the temptation of doing what is easy at the moment instead of persisting with one's deeper wish and intention.

If one wishes to enter into a union with a genuine commitment to the partner, one offers the partner a binding commitment and does not ask to be free of such a thing. A common argument for cohabitation is that it is ethically superior to marriage because it is a genuinely free commitment without binding formalities. However, if one's wish is to commit oneself, there is no ethical superiority in committing oneself less than one could. Cohabitation is ideal for the partner who is the least committed. It is fine as long as relations are good; when there is tension it is the scoundrel's excuse and the dependant's bane. If cohabitation is accepted as equitable to marriage, cohabitation is likely to advance as the chosen form. If both partners are uncertain about the union, they are both likely to see cohabitation as their prudent choice. If one partner is determined to a lasting commitment but the other partner is uncertain, they are still likely to choose cohabitation since in love relationships the partner who loves the least has more power. In both these cases, the availability of cohabitation as an accepted form encourages unions of weak commitment. Only if both are equally determined to a lasting commitment does marriage become the likely choice. If society is neutral on cohabitation versus marriage, it is encouraging unions of weak commitment. If it supports marriage over cohabitation, it is giving unions of strong commitment selective advantage over unions of weak commitment.

With the right of divorce as a unilateral decision, divorce has become too easily available. With cohabitation, there is not even a concept of divorce left. When it becomes an easy and expedite decision to leave a union, it becomes difficult to sustain the very idea of unions as binding commitments.

Postscript: abortion

Do we, in fact, hold the view that abortion is morally problematic and always a grave moral decision? Many no doubt do, but I think it is doubtful that we can claim this to be the prevailing view in contemporary European culture. The terminology of 'free abortion' is not compatible with abortion as a grave moral decision. There is a tendency in medical practice towards easy abortion and to consider abortion among one of several means of birth control. What are we to say about the 'abortion pill'? We know that in some cultures (such as in China and Korea) abortion is used selectively against female foetuses, and even in Europe it is argued that the gender of the foetus should be accepted as a valid reason for abortion (for example, in a recent opinion article in the Swedish daily, *Dagens Nyheter*). In east European countries during the period of communism, the rate of abortion exceeded the rate of live births (in part because contraceptive means were not easily available, but also for deeper moral reasons). In western

Europe, abortion should not be necessary other than in exceptional conditions, but the frequency of abortion is about twenty to 30 per 100 live births. In the United States, the frequency of abortion is about twice as high as in western Europe.[18]

With the right to abortion as an individual decision, it becomes difficult to maintain a constant awareness and debate about abortion as a grave moral decision in relation to the sacredness of life. It is tempting to give in to the view that abortion is a technicality.

Democracy for children

During the second half of this century, Britain has gone through two periods of sharp change in social constellations. The first 25 years were a period of equality with a dramatic narrowing of social differences. The second was a period of inequality with an even more dramatic widening of social differences. Prosperity increased through both periods, but the way that prosperity was shared changed around 1975. In the first period, all groups benefited from economic growth. In the second period, the population divided into winners and losers. Among the losers are children.

Families with children have fallen behind the national average in their standard of living. Child poverty has increased. In a period of rising prosperity, society did not see to it that children were the first to benefit, or even that they shared equally in the fruits of progress. This is not unique to Britain. In the United States, according to statistics published by Congress, poverty ratios among children have increased so that now one child in four lives in poverty. In France, official research (by INSEE) shows that since 1980 the young have been increasingly excluded from the benefits of economic growth.

Protection
One cause of child deprivation is the decline of the stable family household. Single parent families are more likely to be poor; as single parenthood increases, so children are at increasing risk of poverty. No life event has more drastic consequences for the standard of living than divorce; with increasing divorce children are at increasing risk of poverty. The risk of poverty following family dissolution is higher, for

example, than the risk of poverty following unemployment.

A second cause is inadequate economic support to families with children. Child rearing is costly and many parents sacrifice income for the sake of raising children. Economic support nowhere near compensates for the cost and has in many countries (including Britain and the US) been reduced as the cost of child rearing has increased. Welfare states which go to lengths to protect other groups against social risk have not instituted 'social security for children'. In Britain – in this kind and compassionate people – when the social competition intensified, children were not protected against the increasing risk of poverty. We wish the best for our children, but something is not working.

These are only some of several indications that children need stronger protection than they presently have, even in the most advanced and humane democracies. Another indication is violence against and sexual abuse of children, which we are becoming forced to recognise as being not only the actions of deranged strangers, but also as taking place in families as well as in childcare institutions and schools. We do not know if these are increasing problems or if we are simply becoming more aware of them, but we know that they are serious and widespread dangers to children. Yet another indication is suicide. In France, attempted suicide is at its highest level among young persons, in particular girls. In the United States, childhood death rates from diseases have fallen steadily but, since 1950, childhood suicide rates have quadrupled and childhood homicide rates have tripled.[19]

It is deeply disturbing that children do not have better protection, both from the point of view of charity – children are vulnerable citizens – and of efficiency – the future of a society lies with its children. A society that is fair and rational protects its children. Something here is not working: we undoubtedly want protection for children but they are not getting it.

Citizenship

The most important instrument whereby other groups in society have achieved protection against exploitation and abuse is citizenship. In Europe, workers attained full citizenship rights around the turn of the century and thereby achieved protection against exploitation and unacceptable working conditions. Women have attained full citizenship rights in this century and thereby achieved protection against discrimination. Children have yet to attain citizenship.

Children have many more rights today than a generation or two ago, as expressed, for example, in the United Nations Convention on the Rights of the Child and in Britain in the Children Act. Many would no doubt say intuitively that children cannot have the same rights and duties as adults, since they are not fully competent to act independently on their own behalf. It is clearly right that children are not competent to take part on their own in many difficult decisions, but incompetence is not an argument about rights, it is an argument about how to exercise rights. This is gradually becoming recognised, for example, for the mentally handicapped. These citizens are more or less unable to look after themselves and have for that reason long been deprived of basic rights. Modern legal theory is moving to the position that handicapped persons, including the mentally handicapped, indeed do have full citizenship rights and that it is for society to find ways of helping them as best as possible to exercise their rights. It is true that one faces difficult questions about how to do this, that practicable arrangements may be hard or even impossible to find, that help may mean paternalism and that paternalism may easily become dictatorial, but society is not for these reasons justified in concluding that those who cannot speak for themselves cannot have rights.

Voting

The reason we do not have 'social security for children' is that the machinery of democratic politics pays less attention to the interests of children than to the interests of citizens who are voters. The 1997 national elections in Britain followed a period of increasing child poverty. The reason child poverty did not become an election issue is that the workings of democratic politics do not pull the interests of children to the forefront. In the United States, Congress has decided to bring to an end federal programmes of social assistance to poor families with children. It could decide this because democratic politics do not work so as to easily produce protest when the interests of children are being ignored.

Politicians listen to voters. This they do out of necessity. We voters hold the threat of sanction – we can reject our politicians at the next election. Non-voters are not listened to. This is not because politicians are cynical, it is because they must listen to the voters to be elected. Children are not voters. Their interests are not represented by the power of sanction. Parents think of their children when they vote, and politicians know that they do, but parents also have other interests to consider – their own, those of their own elderly parents – and are anyway but a minority in the electorate. Simply, children do not have the power of the vote which would enable them to demand with effect that their interests be respected equally with the interests of others.

Should the political power of children be strengthened by extending the vote to children? If the question appears odd, it might be useful to remember that the extension of the vote to new groups has been the major force in the development and improvement of democracy during the last century or two, and that all extensions have come to be seen as obvious after the fact although before the fact they were all regarded as irresponsible or impossible by those who already had the vote.

Could the vote be extended to children? Again, it might be useful to remember that those against the extension of the vote have always argued that those to whom it might be extended did not have the competence to vote responsibly. Are children competent to vote? Democracies have, in effect, answered in the affirmative by lowering the voting age to include age groups that were previously regarded precisely as children in respect to the responsibility of voting.

However, democracies do maintain that before some age (now usually eighteen) children are incompetent and cannot vote. But incompetence is not an argument about rights, it is an argument about how to exercise rights. Children are citizens. If they cannot themselves exercise citizenship rights, they should have help. If the way we organise the franchise makes it impossible for us to realise the ideal of one person, one vote, and thereby to make the electorate representative of the citizenry as a whole and to assure that all interests are represented by the power of the vote, we should look for a more flexible way of arranging the franchise.

This is the fairness argument. There is also an efficiency argument. Children have a long life in front of them. Their interests lie in the

long-term development of their society. The older other voters are, the more short-term their interests. The exclusion of children from the franchise discourages democratic attention to long-term concerns, such as investment before consumption and environmental protection before exploitation. With the ageing of the population, which European countries are now experiencing, voting power is gradually shifted towards the elderly and away from the young, towards short-term and away from long-term interests.

There are other ways of making the voices of children heard. We could give more support to advocacy groups for children. Schools can arrange informal elections among pupils. In Norway, government has established an ombudsman for children to represent their voice in government planning and political debate. There is also a need to encourage the younger voters today to make use of their vote. However, although giving voice to children is important, only the vote gives citizens the possibility not only to be heard but to be heard against the background of the power to threaten to reject politicians at the next election. Advocacy groups may plead with politicians to listen; voters have the power to force politicians to pay attention.

Not all children can be voters, but with some compromise it is possible to find an acceptable way of extending the vote to the remaining 25 per cent of the citizens who would otherwise continue to be excluded from basic democratic power and representation. This is how:

1. Reduce the lower age of voting to, say, sixteen. This is already in many other respects accepted as the age of maturity.
2. The vote of children who are younger should be exercised on their behalf by custodians. Mothers should be the custodians of the vote of young children. Mothers are often more altruistic on behalf of their children than are fathers and would be more likely to use the vote on behalf of their children than to expropriate it for their own use.
3. Mothers should administer two votes, their own and one for their young children. The second vote should be independent of the number of children. This would prevent the anomaly that many children would give mothers many votes, which might be unacceptable to other voters.[20]

The democratic principle is one person, one vote. Step by step, we have slowly approached this ideal, extending the vote to men without property, then to women, then to the young. We are not yet there, and it matters that we are not; the children remain disenfranchised. The suggested solution for including children in the franchise is not ideal since there can be no presumption that parents and children always have common interests and since also mothers will be inclined to protect their own interests, and have every right to do so. But real democracies are not perfect and do not require ideal arrangements. If the best is not possible, the second best may do and be better than an original situation that has been diagnosed as unsatisfactory.

Appendix 1. Value added in the family economy

Estimates of family economies are drawn from the combined analysis of income data and time-use data. These data sets have been integrated and harmonised for over-time comparability. The estimates cover the ten year period from 1976 to 1986, the first decade in Britain after 1945 of increasing income inequality. More recent data of the necessary quality were not available.

Results (1986 £):

	1976	1986	Growth
Income per person	2675	3515	31%
Consumption per person	6046	7481	23%
Value added	126%	113%	
Persons per family	3.31	3.02	

Population: families in the twenty to 49 age range (head of household), couples and singles, with or without children.

Income: disposable income, after taxes, including state benefits, excluding 'free' services (such as health, education).

Production activities: housework, maintenance and shopping, excluding childcare, other care activities and leisure.

Volume of production: time invested in production activities by adults/parents, excluding the housework of children.
Value of production: the average housekeeper wage (£2.80 in 1986), on the assumption that families 'earn' through their own work what they would have had to pay someone else to do it.

Value added through cooperation is estimated with an 'equivalence scale'. The starting point is a single person household whose (potential) consumption is assumed to be equal to income (including own production as appropriate). If a second person joins the household, it is assumed that less than twice the original income is needed for both to have the same standard of living as the single person had alone. The addition needed for additional adults is assumed to be 70 per cent and for children 50 per cent. Hence, a family of two adults and two children would not need four times the income of a single person but 2.7 times the income. The difference is the value added through cooperation.

Source: Ringen S, 1997, *Citizens, families and reform*, Oxford University Press, Oxford.

Appendix 2. Effects of children on family income

Number of children	Age of youngest child					
	Under 5		5-9		10 and over	
	1986 £s	%	1986 £s	%	1986 £s	%
1986						
Age of head of household: 20-29						
No. children 11937						
One	-3695	(-30.9)	-4470	(-37.4)	-	-
Two	-3729	(-31.2)	-5012	(-41.9)	-	-
Three	-4007	(-33.5)	-	-	-	-
Four plus	-4445	(-37.2)	-	-	-	-
Age of head of household: 30-39						
No. children 13508						
One	-2682	(-19.8)	-990	(-7.3)	-2802	(-20.7)
Two	-2530	(-18.7)	-1964	(-14.5)	353	(2.6)
Three	-3240	(-23.9)	-2051	(-15.1)	-	-
Four plus	-3675	(-27.2)	-4020	(-29.7)	-	-
Age of head of household: 40-49						
No. children 11593						
One	-971	(-8.3)	-2140	(-18.4)	-334	(-2.8)
Two	-847	(-7.3)	567	(4.8)	984	(8.4)
Three	-1527	(-13.1)	361	(3.1)	4541	(39.1)
Four plus	-2980	(-25.7)	-	-	-	-
1976						
Age of head of household: 20-29						
No. children 9608						
One	-2593	(-26.9)	-2005	(-20.8)	-	-
Two	-2682	(-27.9)	-2415	(-25.1)	-	-
Three	-2195	(-22.8)	-	-	-	-
Four plus	-	-	-	-	-	-
Age of head of household: 30-39						
No. children 11059						
One	-2238	(-19.4)	-1497	(-13.0)	-1886	(-16.3)
Two	-2106	(-18.2)	-1465	(-12.7)	-559	(-4.8)
Three	-1785	(-15.5)	-1058	(-9.1)	-	-
Four plus	-1839	(-15.9)	-1062	(-9.2)	-	-
Age of head of household: 40-49						
No. children 9585						
One	-262	(-2.7)	-296	(-3.0)	498	(5.1)
Two	-488	(-5.0)	482	(5.0)	1502	(15.6)
Three	-630	(-6.5)	1186	(12.3)	2583	(26.9)
Four plus	-387	(-4.0)	1740	(18.1)	-	-

Data and population: see Appendix A.

Income: disposable family income, 1986 £s.

The figure after 'No. children' shows the expected average disposable income in the relevant family age category, without children. The other figures show, in absolute and relative terms, the difference between this expected income and the expected income with children, depending on the number of children and the age of the youngest child.

Source: Ringen S, 1997, *Citizens, families and reform,* Oxford University Press, Oxford.

Notes

1. I consistently use the term 'family', but much of what is said about family economics would also apply to various forms of non-family households.

2. There is also the caring of children (unless we have a nanny) and the caring of those who are ill, frail, or old (unless we hire a nurse), which is also production although I here set it aside in order to be as narrowly economic as possible.

3. Some families also have access to 'free services' from government, such as education or health care (which are paid for by taxation but possibly by other families). For simplicity, I do not include services from government in the present discussion.

4. There is also a matter of distribution in the family: not every family member necessarily benefits equally from the available consumption. This difficult issue I have discussed in some detail in Citizens, Families, and Reform. Presently I assume equitable distributions within families.

5. For example, only the value of genuine household work is included, not care work for children or others. Only the work of adults is included, not that of children. The value of household work is estimated with the 'housekeeper wage method', which gives lower estimates than the alternative 'opportunity cost method'.

6. These estimates, as given in Appendix B, result from rather complicated regression techniques of statistical analyses which are explained in detail in *Citizens, families and reform* (Oxford University Press, 1997).

7. In older families with older children, the income effect of children turns from negative to positive. How this may work out over the life-cycle and for life-time income we cannot tell from these date since they only show the situation for different categories of families at the time of observation, and not how the situation changes for the same families over time. These estimates, however, suggest that the positive effect comes late in the life-cycle, that the tendency over time is for it to come later, an that it is not anything near enough to compensate for the negative effect over a long period earlier it the life-cycle.

8. Birth rates in Europe are today alarmingly low from the perspective of population survival. To avoid population decline, a birth rate of about 2.1 children per woman is needed. The average birth rate in Europe is now about 1.5, and some populations seem to be giving up on having children (for example, a birth rate of 0.8 in the former East Germany). If today's birth rates were to persist, and other demographic trends were to remain stable, the European population in 100 years would be less than half of what it is today.

9. The modern demographic transition in Europe towards today's low birth rates has occurred in two steps. First, a reduction in the average number of children born to each woman. Second, a reduction in the proportion of women having children. In Britain, for example demographers believe that the proportion of women who will remain childless is increasing to 20 or 25 per cent of all women. (National Population Projections, Office of Population Censuses and Surveys,

1993.)

10. Obviously, if there is no conflict rules are not needed. It is for protection when conflict arises that there is a need to regulate institutions. Regulations may also help to prevent conflict since rules tell people what there is no use entering into conflict about.

11. I use the term 'contract' as it is commonly used in political theory, as a mutual understanding about rights and duties. Lawyers may dispute whether marriage is a contract (although in French law, for example, marriage law is in the category of contract law). My concern is not with contract formality, but with the reality that couples commit themselves to each other, in principle for life, and that they commit themselves to the shared experience of having children.

12. I do not consider families with more than two adults or with two adults of the same gender, although these could probably be treated under the same logic without much difficulty. Decisions about divorce and abortion may affect more persons than those I consider – the parents of the

couple, children who have moved out, grandchildren, other relations, friends – but I do not consider interests other than those of the immediate family members.

13. Theoretically, there is also the possibility of 'divorce' between children and parents, which is indeed a real issue if we accept that the family is a society of citizens, but I limit my discussion to divorce in the conventional meaning.

14. Dworkin R, 1993, *Life's Dominion*, HarperCollins, London, 32-34.

15. See note 14.

16. 'Two Concepts of Liberty', in Berlin I, 1969, *Four Essays on Liberty*, Oxford University Press, Oxford.

17. See note 14, 17-18.

18. United Nations, 1992, *Abortion Policies*, Vol. I-III, United Nations, New York and Geneva.

19. Children fourteen and younger. Statistics from the Centers for Disease Control and Protection.

20. It would also make the extension of the vote to children possible in populations in which the age distribution is such that children are a majority.